GRASSLANDS
AND
SAVANNAS

ENDANGERED
BIOMES

DONNA LATHAM

Nomad Press
A division of Nomad Communications
10 9 8 7 6 5 4 3 2 1

Printed by Regal Printing Limited in China,
June 2011, Job Number 1105033
ISBN: 978-1-936313-51-8

Educational Consultant, Marla Conn

Questions regarding the ordering of this book should be addressed to
Independent Publishers Group
814 N. Franklin St.
Chicago, IL 60610
www.ipgbook.com

Nomad Press
2456 Christian St.
White River Junction, VT 05001
www.nomadpress.net

Image Credits

Corbisimages.com/ Joseph Sohm/Visions of America, cover

©iStockphoto.com/ Jason Prince, title page; Jussi Santaniemi, 1; Jay
Rysavy, 1; kertlis, 3; ziggymaj, 4; Gerad Coles, 5; Michel de Nijs, 7; Eric
Eisnaugle 8; Eric Isselée, 8, 15, 26, 19; Eneri LLC, 9; Alasdair Thomson, 9;
Johan Swanepoel, 9; kawisign, 9; Le Do, 10; Jeff Goulden, 10; Milous, 11;
DaddyBit, 12; millionhope, 12; Ken Canning, 13; Henk Bentlage, 13; 1 design,
14; Gansovsky Vladislav, 14; Leslie Banks, 14; Marshall Bruce, 15; Sheldon
Kwong, 15; Graeme Purdy, 16; Johan Swanepoel, 16; Alexey Nazarov, 17;
Valentin Casarsa, 17; Stefan Ekernas, 18; Christophe Cerisier, 20; Taalvi, 20;
mypokcik, 20; 1 design, 21; Rich Phalin, 22; YinYang, 24; seraficus, 25.

CONTENTS

What Is a Biome?

Grab your backpack! You're about to embark on an exciting expedition to explore one of Earth's major **biomes**: the grasslands!

A biome is a large natural area with a distinctive **climate** and **geology**. The desert is a biome. The forest, ocean, and tundra are biomes. So are grasslands. Biomes are the earth's communities.

Did You Know?

Scientists don't agree on how many biomes there are. Some divide the earth into five biomes. Others argue for 12.

biome: a large natural area with a distinctive climate, geology, and set of water resources. A biome's plants and animals are adapted for life there.

climate: average weather patterns in an area over many years.

geology: the rocks, minerals, and physical structure of an area.

biodiversity: the range of living things in an ecosystem.

adapt: changes a plant or animal makes to survive in new or different conditions.

ecosystem: a community of living and nonliving things and their environment. Living things are plants, animals, and insects. Nonliving things are soil, rocks, and water.

environment: everything in nature, living and nonliving.

Each biome has its own **biodiversity**, which is the range of living things **adapted** for life there. It also contains many **ecosystems**. In an ecosystem, living and nonliving things interact with their **environment**.

Teamwork keeps the system balanced and working. Earth's biomes are connected together, creating a vast web of life.

2

Landscape and Climate

Trek through the earth's grasslands and you'll find yourself walking across every continent except Antarctica. Grasslands are huge areas of open land with few trees or large shrubs. Grasses cover the vast hills and **plains**.

About one quarter of the earth's land is covered with **temperate** or **tropical** grasslands.

Temperate grasslands are usually in the middle of continents, north of the **Tropic of Cancer** and south of the **Tropic of Capricorn.** They have a growing season in the hot summers and a **dormant** season during the cold winters. Tropical grasslands, near the equator, have a rainy season and a dry season.

of the Grasslands and Savannas

plains: a large, flat expanse of land.

temperate: climate or weather that changes with the seasons but is generally not too extreme.

tropical: climate or weather that is hot and humid all year.

Tropic of Cancer: a line north of the equator. It marks the farthest north that the sun can appear directly overhead at noon.

Tropic of Capricorn: a line south of the equator. It marks the farthest south that the sun can appear directly overhead at noon.

dormant: when plants are not actively growing during the winter or when it is very dry.

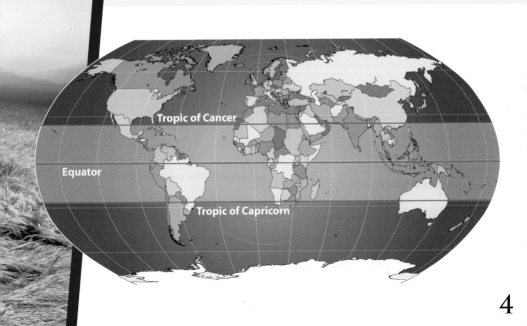

Tropic of Cancer

Equator

Tropic of Capricorn

A temperate grassland does not get enough rain to support a forest. But there is enough rain so it does not become a desert.

Temperate grasslands receive 10 to 35 inches of **precipitation** a year (25 to 89 centimeters). Most of it falls in the late spring and early summer. Summer temperatures can be over 100 degrees Fahrenheit (38 degrees Celsius). Winter temperatures can be as low as -40 degrees Fahrenheit (-40 degrees Celsius).

Grasslands in different places have different names. The United States' and Canada's temperate grassland is known as the **prairie**.

Words to Know

precipitation: any falling moisture, such as rain or snow.

prairie: the temperate grassland of North America.

pampas: the temperate grassland of South America.

veldt: the temperate grassland of southern Africa.

Eurasia: the land that includes Europe and Asia.

steppe: the temperate grassland of Eurasia.

The prairie is generally covered with tall grasses and fills in the land east of the Rocky Mountains.

South America's largest grassland is called the **pampas**. It covers parts of Argentina, southern Brazil, and most of Uruguay. The temperate grasslands of southern Africa are called the **veldt**.

Eurasia's temperate grassland is called the **steppe**. It is the largest grassland in the world, crossing Mongolia, Siberia, Tibet, and China. The steppe is generally covered in short grasses.

Word Exploration

The word "veldt" means "field" in Afrikaans. Steppe means "grassy plain" in Russian.

The **savanna** is the tropical grassland that covers almost half of Africa. Parts of tropical Australia, South America, and India are also covered with savannas.

These are the grasslands near the equator, between the Tropic of Cancer and the Tropic of Capricorn, where it's hot all year.

Temperatures rarely fall below 64 degrees Fahrenheit (18 degrees Celsius), and it can be as warm as 100 degrees Fahrenheit (38 degrees Celsius).

Tropical grasslands receive more rain than the temperate grasslands. That's why there are more trees. The average rainfall is 25 to 60 inches per year (64 to 152 centimeters). Winter is a long, dry season. Summer is wet, with afternoon rains that pour down for hours.

Baboon

here: Temperate grasslands have almost no trees.

there: Tropical grasslands have some scattered shrubs and trees. The acacia tree rises above the savanna grasses.

Acacia tree

Plants Growing in the

Grasses are adapted to the windy environment of wide-open spaces. Their flexible stems bend easily in gusting winds. Built to survive **drought**, thin grass leaves don't lose a lot of moisture when it's dry and windy.

Roots extend deep into dark soil, seeking out water supplies. When wildfires burn above ground, these roots survive below. Then they can **sprout** and grow again. Deep roots also prevent hungry **herbivores** from completely pulling grasses out of the ground.

Springbo

Words to Know

drought: a long, dry period of time, without rain.

herbivore: an animal that eats only plants.

sprout: when a plant sends out new growth.

Wildebeest

Grasslands and Savannas Have Adapted

Did You Know?

Wheat is one of the world's most popular grains. It comes from a grass that grows in grasslands.

Baobab tree

How do trees on the savanna survive wildfires?

Some have **fire-resistant** trunks. Africa's baobab tree is adapted with a huge, spongy trunk. Its thick, crinkly folds protect the tree against fierce flames. During the rainy season, baobabs soak up water and stash it for droughts.

Words to Know

fire-resistant: something that doesn't burn.

evergreen: a tree that keeps its leaves or needles throughout the year.

A large bush called the Ombu is the only tree-like plant that grows on the pampas. It doesn't need a lot of water to survive. The Ombu is an **evergreen** with an umbrella-like canopy that can grow to 50 feet wide and 60 feet tall (15 meters wide and 18 meters tall).

Fire is important in the savanna to preserve its biodiversity. The dry season and its wildfires is followed by the rainy season and new plant growth.

Rhea

now: In the spring, prairies are famous for their colorful flowers like the magenta blazingstar and the purple coneflower.

then: In the fall, the prairie grasses turn yellow, orange, and tan.

12

Animals Living in the

Life in wide-open spaces is dangerous. Unlike creatures in forest biomes, grassland animals can't climb trees to escape **predators**. How have they adapted? Some dig. Prairie dogs, native to North America, tunnel extensive burrows.

Prairie dog

When a predator such as a bobcat or badger slinks up, the prairie dog dashes below ground to safety.

Bobcat

Antelope, bison, and horses are **mammals** with hooves. Hooves are adaptations for tromping through tall grasses. A hoof is actually an oversized toenail. It's a thorny, scaly covering that protects the foot.

Grasslands and Savannas Have Adapted

Words to Know

predator: an animal that hunts another animal for food.

mammal: an animal (including a human) that has a backbone, drinks milk from its mother, and has hair.

species: a type of animal or plant.

graze: to eat grass and other plants in a field or grassland.

With over 40 different **species** of hoofed mammals, the African savanna is home to some of the world's most famous animals. These include elephants, giraffes, rhinos, zebras, lions, hyenas, and warthogs. But **grazing** animals in wide-open savannas are easy targets for sneaky predators.

Bison

Zebras find safety in numbers. A group is called a dazzle because their black-and-white stripes blend into one dizzying mass. This **camouflage** confuses the lion, who can't tell one zebra from another.

Lioness

What Eats What?

Ferocious **carnivores**, such as cheetahs, leopards, and lions, top the **food chain** in the African savanna. They hunt springbok, wildebeest, zebra, and other herbivores with hooves. Hawks snatch smaller **prey**, including meerkats and rodents, as they scurry through grasses. Vultures swoop from the sky to eat **carrion**—if they don't have to share the leftovers with a hyena.

Leopard

Bull snake

Hyena

Words to Know

camouflage: colors or patterns that allow a plant or animal to blend in with its environment.

carnivore: an animal that eats only other animals.

food chain: a community of animals and plants where each is eaten by another higher up in the chain.

prey: animals hunted by other animals.

carrion: the dead and rotting body of an animal.

Giraffe

Cheetah

Gazelles, antelopes, and giraffes use long legs to sprint from roaring lions, wild dogs, and even fires. It's hard to outrun the spotted cheetah, though. This big cat is the world's speediest land mammal. It's capable of running 70 miles per hour (113 kilometers).

Did You Know?

Many animals in the savanna have their babies after the rainy season's new plant growth. All the grass means plenty of food.

16

Environmental Threats

The major threat to grasslands comes from people.

Habitat destruction

occurs when people take over the land in a biome. Because grasslands are flat and **fertile**, they're the perfect **habitat** for farming and grazing cattle.

Today only 1–2 percent of the prairie survives in its original state.

Much of the land is used to grow **crops** such as corn and soybeans. Spreading cities and towns cover the prairie land too.

Grasslands all over the world are used by large ranches to graze their herds of cattle. **Overgrazing** by cattle reduces the amount of vegetation for **wildlife**.

Meadowlark

Words to Know

fertile: land that is good for growing plants.

habitat: a plant or animal's home.

crop: plant grown for food or other uses.

overgrazing: when animals eat plants faster than they can grow back.

wildlife: animals that live in the wild.

cultivate: to plow land and grow crops on it.

Climate change threatens every biome on our planet, including grasslands. **Cultivating** the land during dry seasons or overgrazing makes grassland vulnerable to dust storms. This kind of destructive farming is causing more and more grassland to turn into deserts, called desertification. Huge areas of the African savanna are lost to the Sahara Desert every year because of overgrazing and farming.

Most of the pampas has been cultivated. What used to be called an ocean of grass is now one of the most endangered habitats on Earth.

Biodiversity at Risk

Loss of habitat threatens all species that live in grasslands. More and more animals of the grassland are found only in zoos.

One of the greatest risks to the biodiversity of the savannas is the **poaching** of animals. Poaching can lead to **extinction**. The savanna contains many endangered animals. Although laws protect endangered animals, some people disobey the laws to make money.

People hunt elephants and rhinoceroses for their valuable tusks and horns. Many animals, such as the leopard, are hunted for their skins. Sometimes hunters set fire to savannas so it's easier to spot their prey.

Leopard

Words to Know

poaching: illegal hunting or fishing.

extinction: the death of an entire species so that it no longer exists.

19

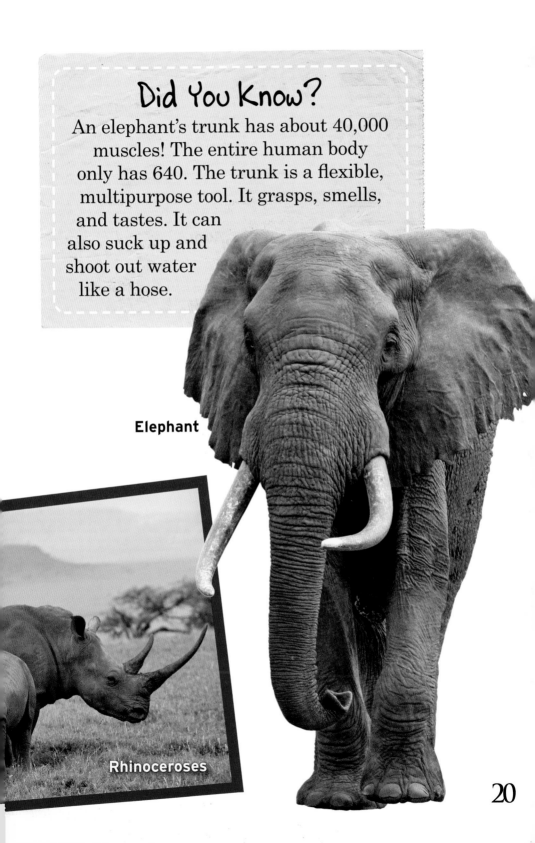

An elephant's trunk has about 40,000 muscles! The entire human body only has 640. The trunk is a flexible, multipurpose tool. It grasps, smells, and tastes. It can also suck up and shoot out water like a hose.

Elephant

Rhinoceroses

20

Path to Extinction

Rare: Only a small number of the species is alive. Scientists are concerned about the future of the species.

Threatened: The species lives, but its numbers will likely continue to decline. It will probably become endangered.

Endangered: The species is in danger of extinction in the very near future.

Extinct in the Wild: Some members of the species live, but only in protected captivity and not out in the wild.

Extinct: The species has completely died out. It has disappeared from the planet.

Red fox

22

The Future of the

Fires, habitat destruction, desertification, and poaching

threaten grasslands and savannas. Each year, more animals of the grasslands are at risk.

People are increasingly aware of the delicate balance of life on Earth. Many are devoted to conserving our natural resources and preserving our biomes.

National parks and game preserves can keep land in its natural state. Preserving habitat allows animals to live in the wild. Kruger National Park in South Africa was established in 1898 to protect the area's wildlife.

Grasslands and Savannas

Conservation Challenge

Think about what You can do to benefit the environment. Inspire others to pitch in. When you use less, every little change adds up to a major impact.

- Did you know most lawns contain non-native grasses? They use a lot of resources to maintain because they need frequent mowing and loads of water. Create your own ecosystem. Plant a yard with native grasses and wildflowers that are adapted to live in your biome.

Don't buy anything made from endangered species. Avoid items created with ivory, feathers, and fur.

- The Environmental Protection Agency (EPA) reports that Americans throw out a quarter of their food. That's 96 billion pounds (44 billion kilograms) of food waste. For one week, weigh the amount of food your family throws in the garbage. Rally everyone to rethink what you dump. For example, can you blend smoothies with mushy bananas instead of pitching them?

- Save energy—and money. Wash clothes in cold water and line-dry instead of switching the dryer on. Your clothes will fade less and last longer. And your impact on the environment will be smaller.

Glossary

adapt: changes a plant or animal makes to survive in new or different conditions.

biodiversity: the range of living things in an ecosystem.

biome: a large natural area with a distinctive climate, geology, and set of water resources. A biome's plants and animals are adapted for life there.

camouflage: colors or patterns that allow a plant or animal to blend in with its environment.

carnivore: an animal that eats only other animals.

carrion: the dead and rotting body of an animal.

climate: average weather patterns in an area over many years.

crop: plant grown for food or other uses.

cultivate: to plow land and grow crops on it.

dormant: when plants are not actively growing during the winter or when it is very dry.

drought: a long, dry period of time, without rain.

ecosystem: a community of living and nonliving things and their environment. Living things are plants, animals, and insects. Nonliving things are soil, rocks, and water.

environment: everything in nature, living and nonliving.

Eurasia: the land that includes Europe and Asia.

evergreen: a tree that keeps its leaves or needles throughout the year.

extinction: the death of an entire species so that it no longer exists.

fertile: land that is good for growing plants.

fire-resistant: something that doesn't burn.

food chain: a community of animals and plants where each is eaten by another higher up in the chain.

geology: the rocks, minerals, and physical structure of an area.

Glossary

graze: to eat grass and other plants in a field or grassland.

habitat: a plant or animal's home.

herbivore: an animal that eats only plants.

mammal: an animal (including a human) that has a backbone, drinks milk from its mother, and has hair.

overgrazing: when animals eat plants faster than they can grow back.

pampas: the temperate grassland of South America.

plains: a large, flat expanse of land.

poaching: illegal hunting or fishing.

prairie: the temperate grassland of North America.

precipitation: any falling moisture, such as rain or snow.

predator: an animal that hunts another animal for food.

prey: animals hunted by other animals.

savanna: tropical grassland.

species: a type of animal or plant.

sprout: when a plant sends out new growth.

steppe: the temperate grassland of Eurasia.

temperate: climate or weather that changes with the seasons but is generally not too extreme.

Tropic of Cancer: a line north of the equator. It marks the farthest north that the sun can appear directly overhead at noon.

Tropic of Capricorn: a line south of the equator. It marks the farthest south that the sun can appear directly overhead at noon.

tropical: climate or weather that is hot and humid all year.

veldt: the temperate grassland of southern Africa.

wildlife: animals that live in the wild.

Further Investigations

Cherry, Lynn. *How We Know What We Know About Our Changing Climate: Scientists and Kids Explore Global Warming.* Dawn Publications, 2008.

Latham, Donna. *Amazing Biome Projects You Can Build Yourself.* Nomad Press, 2009.

Reilly, Kathleen M. *Planet Earth: 25 Environmental Projects You Can Build Yourself.* Nomad Press, 2008.

Rothschild, David. *Earth Matters: An Encyclopedia of Ecology.* DK Publishing, 2008.

Smithsonian Institution National Museum of Natural History
www.mnh.si.edu
Washington, D.C.

US National Parks www.us-parks.com

Enchanted Learning, Biomes
www.enchantedlearning.com/biomes

Energy Efficiency and Renewable Energy
www.eere.energy.gov/kids

Geography for Kids www.kidsgeo.com

Inch in a Pinch: Saving the Earth
www.inchinapinch.com

Kids Do Ecology
www.kids.nceas.ucsb.edu

Library ThinkQuest
www.thinkquest.org

National Geographic Kids
www.kids.nationalgeographic.com

NOAA for Kids
www.oceanservice.noaa.gov/kids

Oceans for Youth
www.oceansforyouth.org

The Nature Conservancy
www.nature.org

World Wildlife Federation
www.panda.org

Index